Table of Contents

Introduction

We became interested in Dog Carting in the early part of 1973 when we went to Florida for the Winter Show Circuit and saw Vince Fiorino's Dog Cart which was made to look like a sulky used in Harness Racing.

We were not interested in riding behind our dogs and having them pull us around, but wanted a utility type cart that we could use to haul things. We searched through all the magazines we could find and could not find anyone that sold a utility type dog cart.

It became obvious that if we wanted that type cart we would have to build one from scratch. The first step was to find out how to make a proper harness for our Giant Schnauzers, and then how to build a workable dog cart.

My wife and I spent many hours in the library looking through books and magazines hoping to find some article on the subject of Dog Carting and construction of a cart and harness.

After several evenings of research we came upon an article written in the Christian Science Monitor in 1942. We also discovered a very informative article written in 1938 by W. Ben Hunt in the magazine Industrial Arts and Vocation Education. He had very excellent diagrams on how to make harnesses that could be used to pull a number of types of devices ranging from carts to travois. He even had diagrams on how to make backpacks.

Armed with our new found information we set about to make our first harness and dog cart. The harness was made out of seatbelt nylon that I was able to purchase from a friend that made car seats for babies.

The cart was made from two x four lumbers for the undercarriage and sixteen inch bicycle wheels. The box of the cart was made with a plywood base and one by four   pine sides. I also made removable racks like the ones they have on the Red Flyer wagons.

The first attempt at carting was almost a disaster for our Giant Schnauzer because we just hooked her up to the cart and told her to heel. She moved a few feet and noticed that something was behind her. She tried to turn to look at the object but was prevented from doing so by the shafts.

She tried to duck under the shafts, but the harness prevented that, so she decided to run away from it and jump over the fence!

The poor dog became stuck on the top of the hedges growing along the fence with the cart hanging beneath her. So much for my first attempt to teach my dog to pull a cart!

Another problem that became apparent as we progressed with our training was that the dog was pulling up hill against the cart because the box of the cart was not on the same plane as the height of the dog.

The shafts were not level with the pulling plane of the dog but were pointing up hill. We had to design a new type undercarriage for the cart and use bigger wheels.

As we progressed in our attempts to design a proper dog cart, we came to realize that each cart should be made to fit the dog, just as each harness should be made to fit the dog. We could make the harness so that there were adjustments possible and the cart so that the shafts could be adjusted to the width of the dog.

The training program evolved over the years and many of our carting friends kept after me to write a booklet on how I train my dogs to pull a cart. The following is my effort to satisfy that request.

History of Program

Training a dog to pull a cart has its origins in history. Early Man first used the dog to hunt for food and guard his possessions. He then discovered he could train the dog to carry loads in backpacks and pull loads on a device called a Travois.

When wheels were invented the dog found itself pulling crude carts for his master. As man developed and made better carts, the dogs work became somewhat less burdensome, but the carts and harnesses remained rather crude until the last part of the Twentieth Century.

Training programs for dogs ere just as slow to develop. The purpose of this Document is to teach you how to train your dog to pull a Dog Cart.

But before you hook your dog up to a cart, there are certain behavior responses your dog must be trained to execute. In order for you to train your dog in Carting, we will first instruct you on the training system we use to teach the dog.

Obedience training as we know it today was started by the Germans around the time of the First World War. The Germans wanted to use dogs for various wartime functions, and as such developed a method to train. This method was soon adopted throughout the world and became accepted as "THE" method to train dogs.

The training was very harsh and disciplined and required physical control over the animal by use of various mechanical collars now known as choke collars, pinch collars or spiked collars.

They were designed to tighten around the dogs throat, causing pain or discomfort at least.

Anytime the dog did not respond correctly or quickly to a command, the lead was jerked or pulled thus causing the collar to tighten and cause pain.   Pain was the motivational stimulus used to cause the dog to learn.

This form of Aversion Training continues to this date and is the most common form of training used for canines.

Modern day psychology, and in particular Educational Psychology has discovered that rather than aid learning, pain retards it, causes stress and makes learning very difficult, if not impossible in some cases.

The anticipation and experience of pain causes the nervous system to react in a negative manner and causes the brain to give off endorphins which in turn help the body lessen the severity of the pain. The brain is more concerned with fighting the pain than with the learning process.

Animal Behaviorists began working with marine animals in such places as Sea World and the United States Navy which was trying to develop a program using Dolphins to aid Navy Frogmen and Disaster Programs for Submarines.

The psychologist involved with the programs realized that the method used to train dogs could not be used with marine animals, and that you could not put a collar on a sea mammal and jerk it around the tank or pool.

In fact, they soon learned that any pain inflicted on the animal resulted in retaliatory behavior. Thus a totally new type of training had to be developed if the Animal Behaviorists were to succeed. Operant Conditioning was developed and is "THE" recognized method of training for all marine mammals.

Those of us in the animal behavior field that work with dogs have long been dissatisfied with the aversion method of training for our best friends and have looked to other forms of training. The following is an example of what can be accomplished with this method of training.

Killer Whales have long been trained with a clicker. In fact, Ted Turner of Sea World is currently using the Operant

Conditioning Method of training to teach Killer Whales a new language that can be used by both man and whale.

Ted Turner is also a dog enthusiast and has offered a series of lectures on the application of Operant Conditioning with dogs. I have had the privilege of attending one of his lectures and also learning first hand the application of this method to dogs from Sue Ailsby, a fellow Giant Schnauzer owner, trainer and Canadian Obedience and Conformation judge, who is an Animal Behaviorist.

Applying Operant Conditioning

There has to be a reason for an animal to do a behavior. Dogs, like people do not perform a behavior without a causative factor. Once we understand the causative factor behind a behavior, we can begin to modify that behavior.

Dogs do not perform behaviors that have moral judgments attached to them.

Dogs, unlike people, do not make moral judgments. Dogs do not do things to get even, or to make you unhappy, or because they are unhappy with the way you are treating them, or for spite, or to cause you to become angry.

Dogs just respond to their basic instincts and training. Moral judgments are the ability of mankind, not dogs.

There has to be a positive reinforcement for the animal to learn. When a dog experiences pain, his reflex reaction is to pull away without thinking.

The dog always wants to please its master, but how can you want to please someone that constantly inflicts pain on you.

With Operant Conditioning you must always make your reinforcements positive, never negative. This leads us to discuss the way dogs learn.

There are two types of behavior. Trained Behavior and Innovative Behavior. Trained Behavior is anything you teach an animal to do for a reward. Innovative Behavior is any behavior initiated by the animal which you in turn reward in order to make it part of the animals behavior repertoire.

In order to teach a dog a behavior, you need to have a training sequence or method.

The sequence used in Focal Training with canines is as follows - **CUE - BRIDGE - REWARD.** A CUE is a sound or action that tells the animal what you want it to do! Hand Cues are part of the action you take to train a behavior. Hand Cues are very important when you

First start training. You can replace a Hand Cue with a Verbal Cue or a Verbal Cue with a Hand Cue. This is done on a gradual basis after the dog has mastered the original Cue.

A BRIDGE is a sound or action that tells the animal it did something right just prior to rewarding it. I use the verbal BRIDGE - Here.   It is important to BRIDGE at the instant the animal starts to responds to your Cue. The timing of the BRIDGE is very important, as soon as the animal starts the desired behavior, you BRIDGE and when the desired behavior is performed you REWARD it.

A REWARD is anything that gives the animal any emotional or physical pleasure. It can be as simple as petting or giving a piece of its favorite food. (Be careful not to overfeed - deduct the amount of food given during training from the animals daily diet.)

Never reward the animal for other behaviors than the one you are teaching.   The animal will incorporate that as part of its behavior pattern (an innovative behavior learning). Keep the bait handy when you train so that the bait is ready to give to the animal when the animal is ready to accept it. Always try to give the bait with your left hand.

The only limit as to what you can teach is your own imagination!

ALWAYS BREAK THE EXERCISE YOU ARE TEACHING INTO ITS SIMPLEST ELEMENTS

Teach the dog those elements step by step. Always work at the animals pace. DON'T WORK TOO FAST. When the animal has done the desired behavior without hesitation, you can proceed to the next step or behavior.

UNLESS THE ANIMAL WANTS WHAT YOU HAVE TO OFFER - DON'T CONTINUE TO TRY TO TRAIN.

Watch the animal's attention span, don't train too long. *

Frustration energizes behavior - as the dog progresses, you can improve its behavior by first delaying the BRIDGE and then delay giving the REWARD.

Dogs tend to anticipate the exercise units and will act accordingly Do not put anything extraneous into an exercise unit as the dog will incorporate it into its behavior pattern. (Innovative Learning.)

If you teach without putting unnecessary stress on the dog, the dog will learn faster - remember longer - perform what it remembers with greater precision.

A CORRECTION is getting the dog to do what you want it to do - NOT punishing the dog for doing something incorrectly.

A CORRECTION is given NOT because the dog did not take the correct action - but because the dog made the wrong decision!

NEVER MAKE MORE THAN TWO CORRECTIONS IN A ROW!

If two corrections are needed, something is wrong; you should go back and teach the exercise again using the units to put the whole thing together!

TRAINING SESSIONS SHOULD BE TEN TO FIFTEEN MINUTES IN DURATION! Each training session should be repeated two to three times a day.

It takes a dog approximately four to five weeks to learn a behavior so that it has command of the exercise in its entirety. Again, the training sequence is: CUE

BRIDGE REWARD

The Magic Button

There have been times when we all wish there was a magic button we could push to turn our beloved pet off when a situation arose that caused the dog to become very excited and noisy and almost uncontrollable!

Well there is such a button!!! Not a physical button, but a word that when spoken by you causes the dog to become calm, quiet, still, controllable, paying attention, doing what you want it to do, rather than acting crazy and uncontrollable.

The magic word is YES! When spoken by you, your dog will listen to you and act in a calm, serene, tranquil, peaceful, placid, composed manner!

How do you get this to work on your dog? You just say the word YES as you give the dog a piece of food. I use small pieces of chicken hotdogs.   My dogs love hotdogs, but you can use any piece of food your dog likes, so long as you can give it in small pieces as you say the word - YES. I just have the dog stand or sit in front of me and give it a piece of chicken hotdog as I say YES.

I do this until I have given the dog the whole hotdog. Cut the hotdog lengthwise into quarters and each quarter into 12 or 13 pieces.

Why does this magic button work so well on the dog? Well, what you are doing is establishing a *conditioned reflex* on the part of the dog to the word YES. You are causing the dog to think of food every time you say YES. It is a physical fact that the dogs body produces the least amount of Adrenalin when it is eating.

When thinking of food the dogs body goes into a set pattern where the blood goes to the stomach and other processes go into effect. Instead of producing Adrenalin, the dog's body produces serotonin, natures equivalent to the drug, Prozac.

The main thing is the dog becomes calm when thinking of food.! That enables you to control the dog, give it a Cue that will bring about desired behavior. YES gets the dog to pay attention to you, acts as a calming agent for the dog. It is a method of telling the dog that all is well. YES is never a command, is never correctable. YES gives you instant control!

After you have taught the dog to respond correctly to YES, you are now ready to teach your dog any other behavior you desire!

The Pack Leader

Every dog owner assumes that when they get a dog that they are going to be the dog's master, because they paid for the dog and they are the owner and are providing food and shelter for the dog. Most of the time their assumption is accurate and becomes reality.

The dog becomes part of the family and looks upon that one individual who cares for it by providing food and water as the leader. Small problems may arise, but in general the young dog accepts every one in the family and at the worse, looks upon the other family members that do not provide food, water and exercising (taking the dog outside to relieve itself) as litter mates.

However, there are times that this scenario does not work out and the dog ends up thinking it is the leader of the group with which it lives.

At this point the dog has become the PACK LEADER and many, many problems arise. The story usually ends with the dog going to the local animal shelter hopefully to be adopted by some unsuspecting new family, or the dog is destroyed if no new owners are found within a reasonable period.

This problem need never arise if the original family that buys the dog follow some very simple procedures that can be practiced by every member of the family and will insure that the members of the family are the leaders and that the dog is subordinate to them.

Dogs have a non-verbal language and as such learn in non-verbal methods. In the wild, it is probable that one animal may learn by imitating another, but this is certainly not a rational process.

Instead, the young may simply follow adult animals and gradually go through the process of performing, practicing and perfecting various behavior patterns.

The Pet Dog does not have pack members to follow and learn from, hence the human family must provide the necessary behavior patterns for the young dog to learn. The following behavior program on the part of the human pack will insure that the dog is able to learn the proper role and live out its life as an acceptable member of the pack that has chosen it.

Another advantage of this behavior program is for the individual who wishes to pursue Obedience Training or competition with their dog. In order for the dog to listen to you, you have to be the leader and have the dog's attention and desire to follow you!

THE PACK LEADER ALWAYS EATS FIRST

In the wild, the pack leader provides the food for the pack by selecting an animal for the kill and leading the pack in the attack and killing the prey animal. After the kill has been made, the pack leader is the first to eat and is able to choose the choice parts of the prey to eat. The subordinates are allowed to eat after the pack leader has made his choice and eaten.

In order to provide the proper role for the young dog you have to assume the position of pack leader and provide the food for the dog. However, there is one more step you have to perform. That is eating first, before the subordinate pack member eats. In order to accomplish this you should eat something before feeding the dog. Eat your breakfast in the morning before you feed the dog. Eat your lunch before you feed the dog, if you feed the dog at mid-day.

Eat your supper before you feed the dog its evening meal, and if you feed the young dog four times a day, eat crackers or something before you feed the dog the last meal of the day.

If you have an older dog, whenever you feed the dog, *eat something* before you feed the dog. This will establish you as the pack leader in the mind of the dog and along with the other behaviors you will be taught to perform, will establish the dog as subordinate to you.

If the dog does not eat all of its food in ten to fifteen minutes, you should pick up the food dish and dispose of the food. Feed the next scheduled meal at the proper time.

THE PACK LEADER ALWAYS CHOOSES THE CHOICE RESTING SPOT

In the wild, the pack leader always gets the choice resting spot. No subordinate would dare to lay on the spot that the leader has chosen for him. This means that you sleep in the bed and the dog sleeps on the floor. In fact, you can provide a spot for the dog to lie, such as a blanket or pillow and instruct the dog to lay on that spot.

You are the pack leader and are picking the sleeping area for the subordinate pack member. The dog should not be permitted to sleep on the bed with a child, because this will make the child a litter mate in the mind of the dog.

This will put the child in a position to have the dog treat it as a litter mate and engage in all the types of play activity that go on between littermates.

Many times the problem of a dog mouthing a child or pulling on the child's clothing or jumping on the child is a result of the dog looking upon the child as a littermate to play with, rather than a higher ranking pack member.

THE PACK LEADER ALWAYS GOES FIRST

In the wild, the pack leader leads the pack in a physical sense. This means that when the pack is moving, the pack leader is leading where the pack is going. It is the pack leader that decides where the pack travels. In the pack you are leading it is important that you always go first.

Never let the dog go through a doorway before you. If you are going down the steps, make the dog follow you down the steps, not go first. If you are going down the hallway, make the dog follow you down the hallway, not go first.

The pack leader goes first! If the dog is lying in the door way and you want to go through the doorway, do not step over the dog or walk around the dog, gently nudge the dog with your toe and make the dog move out of the pack leaders way!

THE PACK LEADER ALWAYS MAKES EYE CONTACT FIRST

In the pack, the leader always initiates eye contact with subordinates and will stare at the subordinate pack member until that member turns his gaze away from the pack leader. In order to teach this to your dog, take a piece of food in your left hand and hold it against your left cheek just under your left eye and say" watch me".

When the dog looks up at the piece of food make eye contact and hold it until the dog looks away. As soon as the dog looks away give it the piece of food as a reward. Practice this at least three times a day for several months until your position of pack leader is well established.

THE PACK LEADER ALWAYS MAKES THE SUBORDINATE EARN ATTENTION

The pack leader never initiates attention with subordinates. The subordinates come to the leader and lick his muzzle and groom the leader. The dog must earn attention - rewards - from you as the leader. When the dog comes to you for attention, you must make the dog earn the attention by doing something for you.

Give the dog a behavior to perform such as "SIT" or "DOWN". Everything the dog does for attention must be controlled by the leader. Do not initiate physical contact with the dog. Let the dog come to you for attention, and make the dog earn the attention you give it.

THE PACK LEADER ALWAYS IS THE BOSS

The pack leader never lets a subordinate get away with anything. This would undermine his authority with the pack. Any member of the pack that gets out of line gets the wrath of the leader. In most instances a brief, furious assault takes place with fur flying, but no serious harm inflicted on the subordinate.

This means that when you give the dog a behavior to perform, the dog must perform the behavior. If you call the dog and tell it to come and the dog does not respond, you must go to the dog and give the dog what is known as a "MOTHER BITCH" correction. Step to the dogs left side and grasp it by the scruff of the neck and shake it three or four times and guide the dog towards you.

Make sure that the dog comes to you. Never tell the dog twice to perform a desired behavior. This teaches the dog that it does not need to listen to you the first time you tell it to perform a behavior. If the behavior you tell the dog is "SIT" the dog must be made to respond to the required behavior even if you have to physically go to the dog and have him properly respond.

THE PACK LEADER ALWAYS WINS THE GAME

The pack leader never lets another member of the pack act as the leader. Therefore when you play a game with your dog, you must always play a game you can win. You, as leader start the game and decide when the game ends. Never let the dog end the game by walking off and doing something else, letting you standing there with nothing to do but go sit down.

When playing chase the ball, watch the dog, and before the dog tires, stop the game by taking the ball and putting it away. Do not play tug of war games with the dog as this is a technique used in agitation training and the dog gets very excited during this type of training and learns to use his mouth in manner that is used in killing prey. In addition, the dog has the ability to keep tugging and you are generally the one that lets go of the article, thus letting the dog think it has won.

THE PACK LEADER ALWAYS HOLDS THE MUZZLE OF THE SUBORDINATE

In the wild, the pack leader will hold a subordinate by the muzzle and make the subordinate submit to the leader. You are the leader when petting your dog. Let the dog know this by putting your hand over the dogs muzzle and gently hold it there.

Increase the time you hold the muzzle until you are in complete control of all parts of the dog's body.

The dog must let you as the leader do what ever you want to do with any part of the dogs anatomy, if its grooming the dog or looking in its mouth or brushing the teeth, or checking the ears. The dog must submit to your control.

This is accomplished on a gradual basis by first getting the dog use to your hand on the muzzle. As you hold the muzzle, gently pet the dog on its neck and back. Do this for a few seconds to begin with; gradually increasing the time you can hold the muzzle. Transfer this technique to other parts of the body, until you have absolute control.

THE PACK LEADER ALWAYS MAKES THE SUBORDINATE ASSUME THE DOWN POSITION

The pack leader always makes its subordinates assume a position that is lower than the leaders. If the leader perceives any act on the part of a subordinate as a threat, that animal is made to assume the down position and expose its belly to the leader. This position is known as total submission.

You must practice making your dog respond to your putting it in the down position and eventually exposing it belly. The down position is a difficult learning behavior for the dog because it is a subordinate behavior. The dog is most vulnerable in this position. Hence, teach your dog the down position and rub its belly at least once a day. It will become pleasurable for the dog and help you to establish your position as leader.

Learn to use every opportunity with the dog to teach the dog you are in command of its environment and that you provide the safe, protective atmosphere the dog desires.

Do not concentrate on stopping inappropriate behavior, but on teaching the dog an appropriate substitute.

Replacement therapy works! Replace undesirable behavior with desirable behavior forget the word "NO"! It only stops a behavior, it does not teach the dog what you want it to do.

Behavior Training

Now that you have your magic button working you are ready to teach your dog behavior patterns. We are going to teach the dog the behavior patterns that will insure that the dog becomes a good companion and family member. These will teach the dog to walk at your side, stand for examination, come when it is called, sit on command and stay and lay down and stay.

A Choke Collar is used in Obedience Training, but during our training, you will work your dog with a buckle collar and a six foot lead to enable you to have control over the dog until it is trained to perform all the exercises with precision and confidence. If you have an enclosed area, you can train the dog free of any collar.

The first behavior pattern we will teach the dog is the SIT. The object of this behavior pattern is to have the dog sit on Cue, wherever the dog is at when the Cue is given. There are two units in the sitting behavior. The first is the dog lifts its head; the second is the butt moves down to the ground.

With the dog standing in front of you take a piece of bait in your left hand and as you put the bait over the dogs head in a slow, steady motion, give the Verbal Cue - Sit. As the dogs head comes up to get the bait, use the bait as a fishhook, keeping it close to the dog's nose, and continue to move the bait above the dogs head.

As the head comes up the dog will do one of two things, either try to step backwards so it can get the bait, or sit and lift its head up to get the bait. If the dog steps backwards, you have moved the bait too fast, and not close enough to the nose.

Keep trying until the dog sits to get the bait. As the dog starts to lift its head to get the bait, BRIDGE (say Here) and REWARD (give the dog the bait). If the dog sat, great. Get the dog to stand and repeat the patter again -Cue - Bridge and Reward.

If the dog did not sit, but just lifted its head, repeat the Cue and try to get the head to come up and the butt to go down. Don't get discouraged it the dog does not sit, but backs up. Move the dog to a wall where it can't back up and try the Cue again. As the dog lifts its head and the moment the rear end starts to go down, Bridge and Reward.

Continue your training for about ten minutes, using the CUE - BRIDGE - REWARD - training sequence! The second behavior pattern we will teach the dog is the COME!

The purpose of this behavior pattern is to have the dog come on Cue and sit directly in front of you with a nice square sit. Have the dog start this lesson from a position sitting directly in front of you.

Take a piece of bait in your left hand and put it in front of the dog's nose. As you give the verbal Cue - COME - take several steps backwards. As the dog starts to get up from the sitting position, BRIDGE and when it gets to your hand, REWARD it.

Your hand should be directly in the center of your body just below your waist. Have the dog SIT and repeat the training sequence. Continue the training for about ten or fifteen minutes. As the dog responds without hesitation to the Cue, increase the distance you move backwards, until you are able to Cue the dog from any distance and have it respond to the Cue without hesitation!

Another method of teaching the COME behavior pattern is to start with the dog sitting in front of you. Kneel on one knee about arm's length from the dog's nose and hold your hand out with the bait just in front of the dog's nose. Give the Cue and move your hand slowly to you so that your hand ends up almost against your chest.

As the dog starts to move towards you, BRIDGE and when it gets to your hand, REWARD. As the dog progresses with this behavior pattern, increase the distance you kneel from the dog and repeat.

This kneeling method is sometimes necessary with timid animals and young animals, allowing you to work on an eye level with the animal. The animal is threatened by the authority figure standing above him and is hesitant to move towards the authority figure.

You can use this position for all of the behavior patterns except the HEEL pattern. In that pattern you can bend as low as possible to encourage the dog to respond satisfactorily. The third behavior pattern we will teach the dog is the **Stand for Examination.**

The purpose of this behavior pattern is to teach the dog to stand still while someone comes up to the dog and examines the dog. The dog must not move its feet during the examination. There is one unit in this behavior pattern. The dog must stand from a sitting position.

Start the lesson with the dog in the sitting position on the left side of your body, dogs head even with your left knee. Take the bait in your RIGHT hand and place it in front of the dog's nose. Give the Cue - Stand - and move your hand a few inches forward. As the dog starts to get up, Bridge and Reward it.

Continue the teaching sequence until the dog responds to the Cue without hesitation. Keep the training session about ten minutes in length.

The fourth behavior pattern we teach the dog is the **FINISH.** The purpose of this behavior pattern is to have the dog move to your left side and sit, from wherever the dog happens to be when you give the Cue - **Side.**

There are four units to this behavior pattern. With the dog sitting in front of you place the bait at the dog's nose level and move your left hand to your left side slowly so as to have the dog stand and move to your left side to get the bait. Give the CUE - SIDE. As the dog moves to your left side to get the bait, BRIDGE and REWARD it. The next unit is to have the dog move to your left rear.

Start the exercise described above and as the dog moves to your left side, move the bait to your left rear (but not behind your back), BRIDGE and REWARD it.

The next unit is to have the dog turn around to the inside. Start the exercise as described and as the dog gets to your left rear, move your hand and the bait to the right and forward so that the dog turns around and is facing forward, BRIDGE and REWARD it. The last unit is to have the dog SIT. Start the exercise as described and have the dog complete all the units before REWARDING the dog.

The fifth behavior pattern we teach the dog is **DOWN**. The purpose of this behavior pattern is to teach the dog to drop to the ground on Cue regardless of where the dog is when the Cue is given.

There are two units in this behavior pattern. Start from the Sitting position with the dog in front of you, keep the bait at nose level and move your hand straight down, close to the dogs chest as you give the CUE - DOWN.

Move your hand down to the dog's feet, and then move the bait forward so that the dog has to stretch forward to get the bait. As the dog touches the ground with its chest, BRIDGE and Reward it. Continue until the dog places its whole body on the ground.

The sixth behavior pattern we teach the dog is **HEEL.** The purpose of this behavior pattern is to have the dog walk at your left side with its head even with your left knee. When you stop, he dog should automatically sit. There are two units in this behavior pattern. HEEL means jump forward and walk at my side.

With the dog SITTING at your left side keep the bait at nose level and run forward a few feet as you give the CUE - Heel. The dog must stand and move forward. As the dog starts to stand, BRIDGE and REWARD it. Keep working on the exercise so that the dog jumps forward when you give the CUE - HEEL. The dog, for the time being in this exercise will only jump forward when you give the Cue. We will put other units into this exercise after we have taught other behavior patterns to the dog.

The seventh behavior pattern we will teach the dog is **BACK UP.** The purpose of this behavior pattern is to teach the dog to Back Up on command from whatever place the dog happens to be. It should back up at least three feet when given the Cue - Back. There is one unit to this behavior pattern.

With the dog standing at your side hold the bait at nose level and move your hand down and under the head to the chest as you give the CUE - BACK. As the dog starts to move back to get the bait, BRIDGE and REWARD it. Does this behavior pattern until the dog moves at least three feet backwards before you REWARD it.

The eight behavior pattern we want to teach the dog is **WATCH ME**. The purpose of this behavior pattern is to teach the dog to look up at you from whatever position the dog is in, Sit, Heel, Stand, or Down. This exercise has one unit. With the dog SITTING at your left side, you give the CUE - Watch Me. As the dog looks up at you, BRIDGE and REWARD it. This behavior can be used in any situation in which you want the dog to watch you.

The ninth behavior pattern we want to teach the dog is the **FRONT.** The purpose of this exercise is to have the dog come and sit in front of you. The exercise has two units. The first unit is the COME. Call the dog to you. As the dog gets to you give the CUE - SIT. BRIDGE and REWARD.

The tenth behavior pattern we want to teach the dog is the **Stay**. The purpose of this behavior pattern is to have the dog stay without moving in what ever position the dog happens to be in. This exercise has one unit. With the dog SITTING at your side, tell the dog DOWN.

Make a fist with your right hand and as you give the Cue - Stay, flash your fingers in the dog's face. Say the word STAY as if it had seven "a's" in it. "Staaaaaaay" Move one step to your right. Remain there for the count of three and return to the dog. If the dog does not stay, say WRONG and repeat the exercise.

Do these behaviors until you have three successful repetitions. Reward each time you return to the dog.

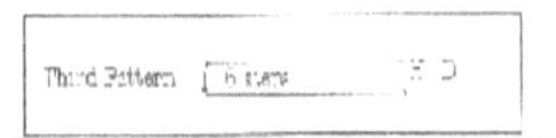

Next move three steps to the right and one step forward and three to the left, returning to the dog's right shoulder. After three consecutive successful exercises, increase the distance to six steps to the right and one forward and six to the left, returning to the dogs right shoulder.

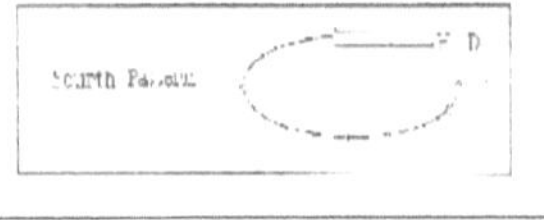

Do these exercises three consecutive times successfully. Practice these drills for a week, three time a day, and then move to the next phrase of teaching the dog to stay. Remember, if the dog moves, say "WRONG" and repeat the exercise.

You should have at least three successful repetitions in a row before you end the training session. With the dog at your side in the DOWN position, say "STAY" and walk six steps to the right and move forward in a curve to the front of the dog. Stand still for a count of ten and follow the same path to return to the dog's right shoulder.

Repeat this exercise until you have three consecutive successful repetitions. Next, do the same pattern, only this time move to the left side of the dog about six steps past the dog.

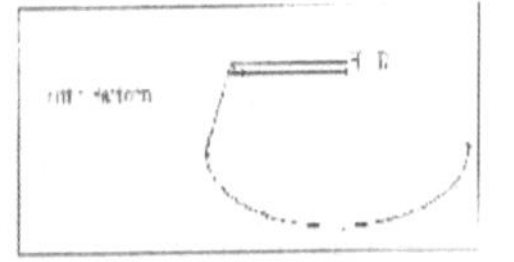

The next pattern is to move six steps to your right and curve around in front of the dog and go six steps to his left shoulder and return on the same path to his right shoulder.

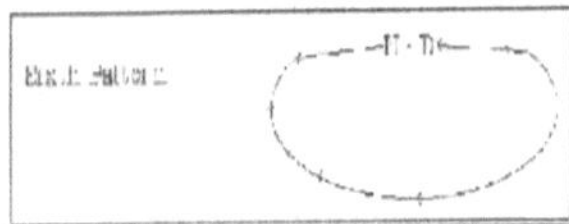

The next pattern is to walk around the dog in a circle ending up at the dog's right shoulder coming to the dog from the rear.

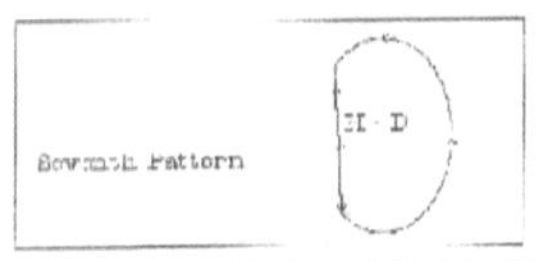

The next pattern in teaching the stay is to walk forward ten steps and face away from the dog so that your back is to the dog.

Remain in that position for ten seconds and return to the dog's right shoulder, walking around the dog as in the above pattern. Reward each time you return to the dog when doing each pattern.

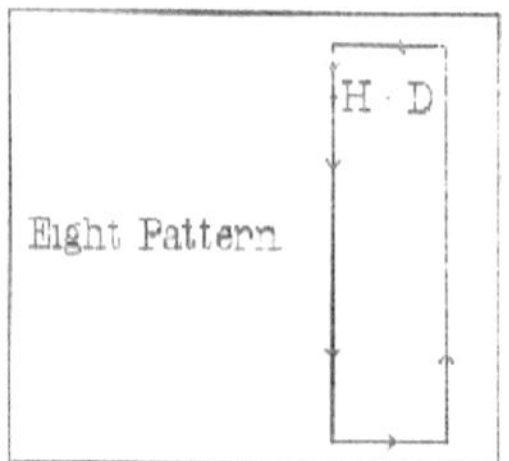

_________________________The last pattern is the same as the above with the exception that you stand facing the dog for the same period of time and then return from the rear to the dog's right shoulder.

After you can successfully complete all the above patterns, repeat them all, increasing the time interval until the dog does the DOWN STAY for at least three minutes. Repeat the training pattern with the dog in the **SIT** behavior pattern.

When successful with that behavior pattern, do it with the Stand behavior pattern.

Putting the Heeling Pattern
Together

Now that your dog has mastered all the above behavior patterns, we are ready to put the Heel pattern together.

With the dog sitting at your left side, give the Cue - Heel, and step forward with your left foot. As the dog gets up to move forward with you BRIDGE. As you move forward, if the dog gets ahead of your left knee, give the Cue - Back. The dog should move back to the correct Heel position.

If the dog starts to drift out to the left give the Cue - Side. This should get the dog to move in to your left side. The Heel pattern to follow is that taught by Dr. Dale Miller in his book "Dog Master". The following diagrams will aid you in your practice of the Heeling pattern.

HEELING PATTERN

ABOUT TURN

START

__________________The next pattern you will learn is the
CIRCLE. This pattern helps the dog to develop a well rounded
personality in his relationship to you, in that the dog learns
that on the outside circle it is more in control, and on the
inside circle, you are more in control, thus providing balance to
the dog,

Practice these circles as follows: do the inside circle and stop at
the center, have the dog sit. Do the outside circle and stop in
the center, have the dog sit. Then do the inside and outside
circle and stop in the center, have the dog sit. This pattern
should be accomplished in less than one minute. Repeat this
pattern until the dog has mastered the pattern.

CIRCLE

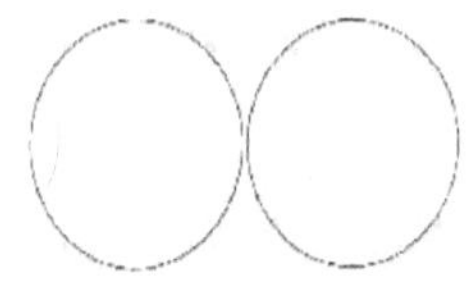

The last behavior pattern you are going to teach the dog is the **FIGURE EIGHT.** The purpose of this behavior pattern is to have the dog walk at the HEEL position moving around people without sniffing or bothering people.

To practice this pattern you need two friends to help you. You can use two garbage cans or other things such as chairs, etc.. Have your friends stand ten feet apart and start with your dog in the center of the area between the two people.

You may go in either direction around the people, making a figure eight as you do so. The dog should walk at the HEEL position and if it gets ahead, give the CUE - Back, if the dog gets wide to the left, give the CUE - Side, causing the dog to move in to your left side. Repeat this pattern until the dog has mastered the pattern.

This is the complete program for NOVICE Obedience. Keep working your dog a few times a day and remember, keep to the program. The dog will learn if you are consistent!!

After your dog has mastered these behavior patterns you should move to a new training place and repeat the training. The fact that the dog learns the lessons in one place does not mean that it will be able to do the behavior patterns in a strange place. In order for the dog to have command of the behavior patterns, it is necessary to teach the complete program in at least FOUR different
places.

This is the complete program for Obedience. Keep working your dog a few times a day and remember, keep to the program. The dog will learn if you are consistent!!

After your dog has mastered these behavior patterns you should move to a new training place and repeat the training. The fact that the dog learns the lessons in one place does not mean that it will be able to do the behavior patterns in a strange place.

In order for the dog to have command of the behavior patterns,
it is necessary to teach the complete program in at least FOUR
different places. Now you have your work cut out for you.
GOOD LUCK!

NOTE: When your dog has mastered the Obedience Training
you are ready to start on the Cart Training.

Teaching Your Dog to Pull a Cart

STEP 1.

Give the Cue - STAND - STAY. Put the harness on your dog.
BRIDGE and REWARD. Adjust the shoulder strap so that it
allows the chest strap to set on the dogs breast bone and not
too high so that it interferes with his throat nor too low as to
interfere with his leg movement.   Repeat this behavior pattern
until the dog is in command of the behavior pattern.

Next, tie the traces over the back of the dog. Cue - HEEL and
walk the dog around with the harness on so that it becomes
use to the feel of the harness. Remember -BRIDGE and
REWARD! Repeat the behavior pattern until the dog has
mastered the behavior.

When this is accomplished, untie the traces and have someone
walk behind the dog holding the traces, applying a small
amount of pressure so the dog becomes use to pushing a little
against the breast band. Remember, Cue - HEEL - BRIDGE
and REWARD!

STEP 2.

GETTING THE DOG USE TO THE SOUND OF THE CART
BEHIND IT

HEEL the dog with the harness on (Cue - BRIDGE - REWARD)
and have someone walk behind the dog pulling the cart.
Repeat this behavior pattern until the dog is comfortable with
the sound of the cart behind it.

REMOVE CART RACKS FROM CART WHILE TEACHING THE
DOG TO PULL

Next, walk the dog to a position in front of the shafts, with the
shafts lying on the ground. Cue - BACK so that the dog backs
up between the shafts, BRIDGE and REWARD. Cue - STAND -

STAY. Lift the shafts so that they are parallel to the ground and let the dog become accustom to the feel of the shafts along side it. BRIDGE and REWARD.

When the dog has mastered this behavior pattern, feed the shafts thru the loops on the harness and let the dog stand with the weight of the cart on the harness. (Cue - STAND - STAY). BRIDGE and REWARD. Remove shafts from the loops by sliding the shafts to the rear. Cue - HEEL - walk the dog between the shafts holding the right shaft in your left hand at correct height - BRIDGE - go five to ten feet, REWARD. Praise the dog all the time. Repeat the behavior pattern until mastered.

STEP 3.

Cue - HEEL. Walk the dog with the shafts in the loops of the harness but not hooked up to the cart. Hold the right shaft in your left hand while doing this. BRIDGE. Again go five to ten feet. REWARD. Repeat the behavior pattern until the dog is comfortable walking between the shafts.

IF THE DOG STARTS TO SHOW FRIGHT AT ANY POINT IN TRAINING - STOP - REMOVE THE CART FROM THE DOG AND LET THE DOG WALK AROUND THE CART WITH THE HARNESS ON, SMELLING THE CART AND EXAMINING THE CART!

STEP 4.

Cue - STAND - STAY - Move cart so that shafts are thru loops on the harness. Hook the traces to the cart! BRIDGE and REWARD. Cue - HEEL - walk the dog forward five to ten paces! BRIDGE and REWARD. Stop and unhook the dog. Repeat this behavior pattern until the dog is comfortable walking between the shafts and pulling the cart! Next have someone walk behind the cart and apply a small amount of drag to the cart in order to provide the feeling of pulling to the dog.

STEP 5.

To teach the right turn it is necessary to work the dog in a large area. Cue - HEEL - move forward slowly and start to lead the dog to the right. BRIDGE. CONTINUE until you have completed the right turn. REWARD. If you turn too tightly, the shafts will bump against the dog and could panic the dog, so go slowly and wide.

Use the same behavior pattern to teach the left turn. Have someone apply drag to the cart while you are teaching the turns.

STEP 6.

Let the dog pull the cart freely on lead. When the dog is comfortable pulling, put the racks on the cart and let the dog pull the cart. (Racks sometimes make noise and scare the dog.)   Add ten pounds to the cart (centered in cart) and train with this weight for one week. Add weight in increments of five pounds. Work with a given weight for four or five days. Make sure not to over do the weight.

Maximum weight should be sixty pounds (60lbs.). Sandbags work well for the weights as they are very easy to handle and will not damage the cart.

STEP 7.

Make left and right turns tighter as the dog progresses! The dog should be able to turn the cart in a 360 degree circle without the wheels leaving an eighteen inch circle.

STEP 8.

Teach the dog the BACK UP. Use the same training pattern as you did in the obedience training. The dog should be able to back up the cart at least four feet in a straight line.

HAPPY CARTING!!!

Conditioning Your Dog With a Cart

Many people use their carts for many things. Giving kids'
rides, marching in parades, cleaning up the yard and carrying
groceries are some of the most common uses people have told
me about. One use that is not well known is using the cart to
condition your dog. This can be done without much effort on
your part, but does demand adherence to a strict schedule.
Our Giant Schnauzer, Cinderella needed better conditioning
than she had. My wife decided to use the cart to condition the
bitch. She spoke to a friend of ours that was involved in
body-building.

The information she received enabled her to develop a
conditioning program for Cinderella. The program consisted of
having Cinderella pull the cart with ten (10) pounds loaded in
the cart on a railroad bed for the distance of one mile. This
was to be done every other day in order to allow the muscles to
rest and rebuild on the off day. The weight was increased every
two weeks by five pounds. We used sandbags for weights and
found this to be very easy to handle and to add sandbags to
increase the weights.

We continued this program until Cinderella was pulling sixty
(60) pounds every other day. It is important that you stay on
schedule and find a dirt, cinder, sand or grassy area to exercise
the dog. We presented Cinderella under Mr. Head, an
Australian judge at the New Brunswick KC show in September,
1978.

She went Best of Breed. Mr. Head asked how we were able to
keep the bitch in such outstanding condition. Of course we
told him about our conditioning program using the dog cart.
He was not familiar with carting and had no idea what we were
talking about. He was very pleased to learn bout carting and
the use we made of the cart to condition Cinderella.

Cinderella was the number one Giant Schnauzer Owner Handled Bitch in the country in 1978 and 1980. Other Giant people have used their carts to condition their dogs. The Alders, Shelly and Marcia, had a Giant named Timmy. Timmy had stepped in a hole while running and had broken his right rear leg.

While the leg mended well, Timmy was left with a slight limp. Shelly Adler, who is a Surgeon, realized the importance of exercise and conditioning and used his cart much in the same manner that Marie did with Cinderella.

The results were outstanding. Timmy became a champion the same day Cinderella earned her championship. Needless to say, the carting conditioning program strengthened the leg and eliminated the limp.

We frequently get calls from people who have shown a Rottweiler under a well known breeder - judge - author who have been informed by the judge that the dog needs conditioning and to contact us about purchasing a dog cart in order to start a conditioning program with their Rottweiler.

In order to have a well conditioned dog, whether you are interested in showing the dog or not, you have to start a program such as described. It is better for the health of the dog and at the same time you get the benefit of walking with your dog which will in turn help improve your health.

Now that your dog can pull a cart and you have practiced until your dog is very proficient, you are ready to enter a carting competition. Many breed clubs have established carting certification and award certificates. The Giant Schnauzer Club of America is one of those clubs. The following routine has been accepted by that Club and is fun to practice as well as practical for your dog to master. Many of the behaviors the dog is required to perform in this routine have been experienced by the writer in my carting experience in the community in which I live.

I use my dogs to do many of the daily things one does such as shopping, going to the lumberyard, gardening, etc.. In fact, one local radio program had a segment it presented every Saturday Night about one of my dogs involved with his cart in the collection of ROAD KILL, which was offered for sale by a Truck Stop Restaurant which used it to make Pennsylvania Road Kill Scrapple. Of course the story and the restaurant were all make believe, but the part about my dog pulling his cart all over town was true and that is what made the story so interesting to the audience. All you need to practice the carting routine is a space forty (40) feet by sixty (60) feet and two posts that can be set up as gates to have the dog pull the cart through.

An eighteen inch circle is used for the circle right and circle left, and can be cut out of a piece of cardboard and spray painted white around the edges to get a perfect eighteen inch circle.

The follow narrative will give you some idea of what is involved in the dog cart judging and what is expected of you and your dog in the routine.

General Comments on Judging Performance and Execution

Each command in carting requiring the dog to move the cart requires some of degree of execution on the part of the dog which affects the movement of the cart and any load in the cart. It is therefore important to note the dogs ability to move the cart without any jerking or lateral movement.

On command FORWARD, the cart dog must be able to move the cart from a standing position without any noticeable degree of sudden jerking forward. This type movement would cause any load in the cart to move towards the rear of the cart thus changing the balance of the load. The cart dog should be able to move the cart forward without any noticeable sudden movement of the cart.

The forward motion should be smooth and effortless. On the command HALT, the cart dog should bring the cart to a smooth stop so that the rings on the shaft do not ride up against the loops of the harness thus pushing the harness forward towards the shoulder.

On the command LEFT TURN or RIGHT TURN, the cart dog should be able to turn the cart in the shortest possible arc. This means the dog must be able to side step while turning. If the cart dog does not side step, but merely walks in a turning direction, the arc will be much greater than if the dog side stepped.

In the FIGURE EIGHT behavior pattern, the cart dog demonstrates the ability to move the cart around people. This ability is necessary when the cart dog moves thru shopping centers and other populated areas.

It is indeed rare that the dog will be able to proceed in a straight line without anyone interfering with his movement. The cart dog is able to recognize and sense the distance necessary to maneuver the cart thru a given space. Thus if the cart dog bumps the post, the exercise is scored a failure or zero.

The BACK UP behavior pattern is the most difficult maneuver the cart dog is called upon to perform. It is necessary for the dog to learn to back-up the cart as there are times when the cart team find it impossible to continue to move forward, and must move to the rear in order to avoid an obstacle and move around it.

The cart dog is judged on the ability to move the cart backwards in a straight line, at least four feet, without turning it over or dumping the load.   (Of course, in competition there is no load in the cart.)

The CIRCLE LEFT and CIRCLE RIGHT behavior patterns demonstrate the cart dog's ability to side step the cart in as tight a turn as is possible.   The ideal is that the inside wheel not move from the spot but merely pivot in place.

The RECALL behavior pattern not only demonstrates the cart dog's ability to come when called, but the agility to move the cart thru a gate with six inches clearance on either side of the wheels. The dog is not guided thru the gate but must maneuver thru the gate on his own.

The FAST and SLOW behavior patterns again demonstrate the cart dog's ability to change pace without disturbing the load.

Carting Competition and Handiness Test

To be judged on rhythm, straightness of tract, smoothness of transition and ease and accuracy of execution. The dog may sit or remain standing on the halt.   The dog may be given verbal commands or hand signals by the handler.   The handler may walk at the heel position or along side the cart. The handler may not touch the dog or the cart.

The CARTING CERTIFICATION EXERCISE is performed only on lead. The ADVANCED CARTING CERTIFICATION EXERCISE is performed off lead.

A. HEELING EXERCISE.

1. The cart dog and handler enter the ring, positioning the team for the first part of the behavior pattern.

a. The judge asks "ARE YOU READY?" Commands FORWARD. After eight or ten paces the command HALT is given. The judge should note the track, position of cart dog to handler, does the handler adjust to the dog, does the team display rhythm and smoothness in stopping.

b. Command FORWARD is given. The team proceeds to the end of the ring where LEFT or RIGHT turn is given - handler may execute the turn with or without command to the cart dog.

c. Halfway across the ring RIGHT TURN or LEFT TURN command is given - after several paces the command FAST is given - then the command NORMAL is given just beyond the halfway point of the ring.

d. As the team approaches the end of the ring, the command LEFT TURN or RIGHT TURN is given.

This takes the team towards the original starting position. The team is then given the command LEFT ABOUT TURN.

This demonstrates the ability of the cart dog to execute an about turn to the dogs left or inside. (DEDUCTIONS ARE MADE

FOR TURNING TOO WIDE.)

After executing the LEFT ABOUT TURN, the command SLOW is given, then NORMAL and at the edge of the ring, the command RIGHT TURN is given.

After several paces the command HALT is given. The command FORWARD is given and at the end of the ring, a command for a RIGHT ABOUT TURN is given. About mid-ring, a LEFT TURN command is given thus positioning the team for the FIGURE EIGHT EXERCISE.

B. The FIGURE EIGHT EXERCISE

a. The cart dog and handler are positioned for the FIGURE EIGHT EXERCISE. The judge states "You may go in either direction". "Are you ready?" The judge commands FORWARD and the team execute the FIGURE EIGHT.

The judge notes the cart dog's ability to go around the posts without bumping either post.

NOTE * In Carting, the stewards should stand fifteen (15) feet apart.

C. THE BACK UP EXERCISE

The handler and cart dog are positioned for the BACK UP EXERCISE. (CART DOG IS REQUIRED TO BACK UP THE CART AT LEAST FOUR (4) FEET.   A TAPE MAY BE LAID ON THE GROUND TO ASSIST THE JUDGE IN MEASURING THE   DISTANCE OR A METAL YARDSTICK IS PLACED TWELVE INCHES BEHIND AND TO   THE OUTSIDE OF THE LEFT WHEEL TO BE USED AS A GUIDE.

The judge asks "ARE YOU READY?" Commands "BACK UP YOUR CART."   (HANDLER MAY NOT TOUCH THE DOG OR THE CART, BUT MAY USE VERBAL   COMMANDS OR HAND SIGNALS.)

D. CIRCLE LEFT EXERCISE

Cart dog and handler are positioned for the CIRCLE LEFT EXERCISE.   (left wheel in center of circle.)

The judge asks "ARE YOU READY?" Judge commands CIRCLE LEFT.   The dog must execute a 360 degree turn keeping the left wheel inside an 18 inch diameter circle.

(DOG TO BE JUDGED ON ABILITY TO KEEP THE WHEEL IN THE CIRCLE.) IF THE WHEEL LEAVES THE OUTSIDE OF THE CIRCLE, THE EXERCISE IS SCORED ZERO. THE JUDGE MAY DEDUCT POINTS BASED ON THE DISTANCE THE WHEEL MOVES FROM THE CENTER OF THE CIRCLE, BUT DOES NOT LEAVE THE CIRCLE.

E. CIRCLE RIGHT EXERCISE

The cart dog and handler are positioned for the CIRCLE RIGHT EXERCISE. Right   wheel in center of circle.

The judge asks "ARE YOU READY?" The judge commands CIRCLE   RIGHT. The cart dog must execute a 360 degree turn keeping the wheel inside an 18 inch diameter circle. (THE SAME CRITERIA APPLIES AS FOR THE CIRCLE LEFT EXERCISE.)

F. THE RECALL EXERCISE

The cart dog and handler are positioned for the RECALL EXERCISE.

The judge informs the handler THIS IS THE RECALL EXERCISE. "ARE   YOU READY?"

On the command LEAVE YOUR DOG, the handler commands the cart dog STAY and proceeds to the gate and removes the bar.

The handler proceeds thru the gate, positioning himself on the far side of the gate with sufficient room to call the cart dog thru the gate. On the judge's command, the handler calls the cart dog. The cart dog must proceed thru the gate without interfering with the gate. The cart dog should come to a halt in front of the handler. (The cart dog may sit or remain standing.)

Upon the judges command EXERCISE FINISHED the handler replaces the bar and returns to the right side of the cart dog by walking around to the right side and stops at the proper position. The cart dog should not move while the handler is replacing the bar and returning to the proper position.

NOTE * When judging carting competition, the judge should use the "Regulations for Performance and Judging" as approved by the American Kennel Club as a guide.

The fact that the dog is working with a cart does not substantially alter the obedience regulations and requirements of performance.

JUDGES SCORING DOG CARTING COMPETITION CHART

On-lead Heeling	20
Figure Eight	10
Backup	20
Circle Left	15
Circle Right	15
Recall	20
Total Points	100
Off Lead Heeling	20
Figure Eight	10
Backup	20
Circle Left	15
Circle Right	15
Recall	20
Total Points	100

CARTING DEMO ROUTINES

If you are not interested in competition with your cart dog, you may wish to join three carting friends and engage in precision drill with your cart dogs.

A few Giant Schnauzer fanciers developed the following routines for Carting Exhibitions.

WEEPING WILLOW ROUTINE

Cart Dogs #1, #2, #3, #4, enter ring in line and go clockwise. #1 will cut up the center of the ring from the side they want to end up facing. #1 and #3go right, #2 and #4 go left around the ring and then come up the center again in pairs.

#1 & #2 go to the far sides and all four come down the ring in a line. Sit the Dogs and wait for applause.

Ringmaster introduces handlers and Cart Dogs starting with #1. (Stand Cart Dog by taking one step forward as you are introduced.)

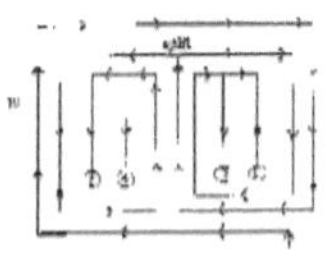

RECALL ROUTINE

#1 & #3 drop off diagonal to where they have been at the end of the recall. #2 & #4 stoop diagonal to where they have been.

2. Ringmaster calls "leave your dog". When Handlers are in line facing dogs, Ringmaster calls "Call your Dog". Dogs come and sit. Ringmaster calls "Return to your dog". Handlers circle Cart and go to the Cart Dogs Right shoulder. Demo continues with #2 leading off Clockwise.

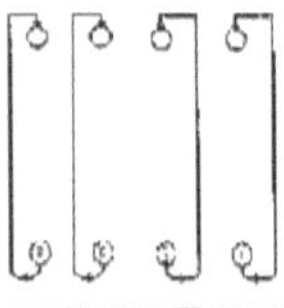

CROSSOVER FROM TWO CORNERS ROUTINE

#1 & #3 drop off diagonal to where they have been at end of Recall. #2 & #4 stop diagonal to where they have been.

2. #1 always moves out first, followed by #2, #3, #4. Turn at your corner, keep moving and do the Crossover again returning to original position shown.

3. #1 & #2 only – cross over a third time to create starting position for next Routine

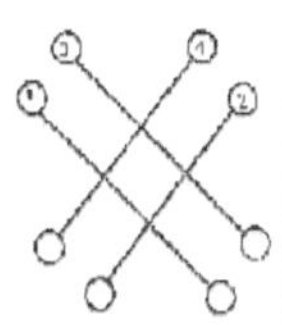

CROSSOVER FROM FOUR CORNERS ROUTINE

In this Routine, two dogs will be crossing simultaneously. Go to the Left so that the Handlers will be between the dogs. #1 & #3 move out together and cross to opposite corners. #2 & #3 do the same seconds later. As they get to their corners, #1 & #3 will have turned around and started the

Return. #2 & #4 do likewise.

When you are back in your original corner, begin moving clockwise to line up behind #1.

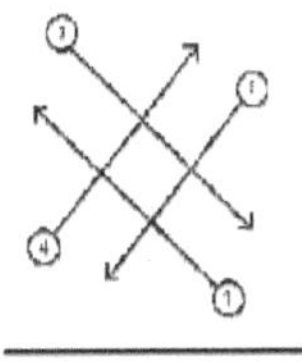

BASKET WEAVE ROUTINE

Note. When you make your turn at the head of the line, go to the left of the cart behind you, then Weave. People coming up the line waiting to turn remain straight.

Routine ends when #1 leads the group clockwise around the ring and begins making smaller circles to start the next formation.

(Banners should be in Banner Routine Cart #2 & #4)

BANNER ROUTINE

When Carts have formed square (diagram shows order Of dogs only, #1 may be at
North, South, East or West Position, depending on when square forms, #1 moves up
alongside #2, #3 moves up alongside #4. Pass Banners. Start moving #1 & #3 out to
the end of Banners, making a full circle so everyone can read Banners and staying
in 180 degree circle.

Move back in #1 going in ahead of #2 and #3 ahead of #4. #1 and #3 put Banners in
Carts.

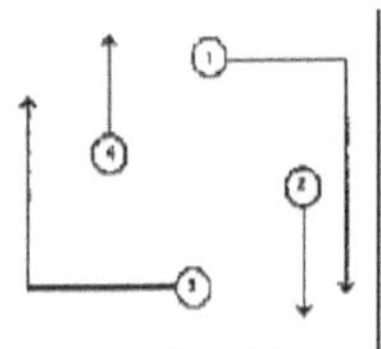

About The Author

I was the Senior Psychologist at a State Correctional Institution when I got my first Giant Schnauzer. I conducted Individual and Group Therapy for a population of over nine hundred fifty individuals.

The Program was successful and I went on to become the President, Pennsylvania Association on Parole, Probation and Corrections. I also became the Regional Director of the Criminal Justice Agency covering fifteen counties in North East Pennsylvania. A position from which I eventually retired.

I was able to utilize my professional training to develop a method of working with dogs. My wife and I competed in both conformation and obedience events. We showed seven generations of Giant Schnauzers to Breed Championship and one to Companion Dog Title. WE became involved in dog carting and manufactured dog carts for over twenty years. I had a dog behavior practice for over thirty years and received many referrals from Veterinarians in North East. Pennsylvania.